THE KREGEL
PICTORIAL GUIDE TO
CHURCH HISTORY

VOLUME 5—THE CHURCH IN THE LATE MODERN PERIOD
A.D. 1650–1900

JOHN D. HANNAH

The storming of the Bastille, Paris, during the French Revolution, 1789.

Kregel
Publications

The Kregel Pictorial Guide to Church History, *Volume 5* by John D. Hannah

Design copyright © 2008 Lion Hudson plc/Tim Dowley Associates Ltd

Text copyright © 2010 Kregel Publications

Published by Kregel Publications, a division of Kregel, Inc, PO Box 2607, Grand Rapids, MI 49501.

ISBN 978-0-8254-2786-2

Worldwide coedition produced by
Lion Hudson plc
Wilkinson House
Jordan Hill Road
Oxford OX2 8DR, England
Tel: +44 (0) 1865 302750
Fax: +44 (0) 1865 302757
Email: coed@lionhudson.com.
www.lionhudson.com

Printed in China

PICTURE ACKNOWLEDGMENTS

Illustrations
Shirley Bellwood: pp. 25, 28 left
David Smith: p. 18
Peter Dennis: pp. 27, 28 right

Photographs
Illustrated London News: pp. 15, 16, 17, 19, 26, 29, 30, 31
Billy Graham Center: p. 22

All other maps and illustrations:
Tim Dowley Associates

Contents

Introduction

The *Modern Age* as an era is difficult to define. There seems to be a consensus, though, that this period has fallen into eclipse or is passing away entirely. By most definitions, the Modern Age was an unprecedented epoch of progress in the natural sciences, but it also produced a trend in the arts to reflect progressive despair. For all its attempts, the humanities addressed but failed to conquer an uneasy emptiness of human soul. As Samuel H. Miller wrote, "If we handled nature like giants, we handled ourselves like idiots" (*The Dilemma of Modern Belief* 1963).

Brave new world?

For some, like novelist Fyodor Dostoyevsky (1821–1881), the contemporary time was a demonic age. For philosopher Friedrich Nietzsche (1844–1900), the time was decadent, but it had potential as the path toward a more evolved humanity. For social historian Oswald Spengler (1880–1936), the Modern Age was the twilight of civilization. For the social-critic novelist George Orwell (Eric Arthur Blair, 1903–1950), it had all the portent of an "animal farm." For poet and literary critic T. S. Eliot (1888–1965), modernity was a wasteland.

Some saw it as the dawn of a new world. Karl Marx (1818–1883) believed that out of the Modern Age would come the age of the proletariat. Walt Whitman (1819–1892) stated a similar thought more romantically, that humanity had entered the era of the common man. In the thought of some political theorists, it was the age of liberty and democracy.

Reason supreme

Advances in the natural sciences conquered some causes of human pain and brought hope for an even better quality of life. But, humanity did not achieve the contentment of a safer, more technologically advanced world. To the contrary, it seemed the soul was emptied of hope, even as promises for a better temporal existence were fulfilled. Reason was the new highest authority, replacing spiritual authority in Scripture and accumulated cultural traditions. The scientific method was used to answer all mysteries. Mind seemed more important than heart. Entertainment came to replace deeper values in determining significance. A culture of human arrogance swept away the need for submission to the divine.

Renaissance and Reformation

The early modern period (1500–1650) was rooted in the late medieval Renaissance. The late modern era drew on the more rationalistic aspect of the Renaissance. A spirit of human independence in revolt against imposed authority characterized both early and late eras of modernism. Reform-minded Christians in the early period opposed authority not granted by the Bible. Reformers sought to place the church on a more certain foundation that was centered in Scripture.

The sixteenth-century Reformers did not intend to overthrow medieval faith in an authority outside humanity. Ultimate truth was found in the Bible, and

normally it still was interpreted by churchmen and tradition. But despite their common medieval heritage, Roman Catholics and Protestants did not come to the same conclusions as they applied authority structures.

Late modernists broke with their predecessors when they set human reason over the authority of Scripture. It was a very different concept that a prosperous and sound human society could be constructed and maintained through reason alone. The new idea was that the authorities of church and state had failed. Now unrestricted authority would be

vested only in the mind. At the same time, other voices argued that, whatever the human basis for authority, utopia could not be expected in a world fallen from grace.

Enlightenment religion

The story of the late modern world grew out of medieval and Renaissance ideas, but its deep roots were in a new view of life as given by the Enlightenment. Enlightenment religion, whether seen through the Roman Catholic or the Protestant lens, involved two perspectives. First, the more popular and influential philosophers questioned or directly assaulted past Christian assumptions. Second, churchmen tried to rescue and preserve the faith from these new questions. In the process, religionists divided between camps that might be described as liberal and conservative or traditionalist. The differences were grounded in respective stands on preserving the faith in an increasingly secular environment. In the new outlook, philosophy had precedence over theology, the natural sciences and natural philosophy over grace, and reason over faith.

Human rights displaced religious creed in a progressively Christless, secularized worldview. It became difficult for those who wanted to maintain a vital faith to know when the quest for relevance began to disfigure the essence of belief. In retrospect, it seems to have been futile to try to preserve Christianity's authority in social and cultural norms by redefining Christianity. The hegemony of Christian faith and values, inaugurated in the fourth century, was crumbling.

The Enlightenment was a death sentence for Christian cultural dominance in the Western nations.

The Enlightenment and the Rise of Skepticism

The Age of Reason

The Age of Reason, as the Enlightenment is sometimes called, came about through a confluence of three phenomena: (1) the emergence of secularized philosophy; (2) the discrediting of revelation and tradition as sources of authority; and (3) advances in the natural sciences. In his *Church Dogmatics*, Karl Barth (1886–1968) described the Enlightenment as a system founded upon the presupposition of human ability.

The world no longer was a mysterious place controlled by an incomprehensible God. Its complexity was governed by intelligible laws. Understanding those laws, humankind could engineer a glorious future. Ancient truths, such as the deformity of human sin, gave way to confidence that education would quiet the beastly side of human nature. Utopia seemed a possibility, whether inaugurated through nationalism or self-struggle. Heaven was no longer the final hope. The Creator who orders all things according to the counsels of his good pleasure was marginalized as an artful watchmaker. After fourteen centuries as society's ultimate source of values and hopes, Christianity was dethroned.

The French rationalists

Called the first modern man for his method of searching out truth, René Descartes (1596–1650) relied on his own reflections over the ancient sources. The revelation of God was not so much available in a book. Rather, God had put it in the mind. François Marie Arouet Voltaire (1694–1778), Jean-Jacques Rousseau (1712–1778), and the encyclopedists epitomized the French rationalist tradition. They allowed the necessity of God's existence, but rejected Scripture as an authority. The argument from design was assumed by Voltaire when he said, "I shall always be convinced that a watch proves a watchmaker and that a universe proves God." Rousseau bid us "gaze upon the spectacle of nature, give heed to the inner voice."

An English empiricist

Englishman John Locke (1632–1704) was a moderate among those who adopted the Age of Reason. He viewed the Bible as the revelation of God but made all authorities, including Scripture, subject to the scrutiny of reason. The axiom of the rationalists was that truth is revealed through the criteria of repeatability and common sense. Locke accepted some

René Descartes (1596–1650).

biblical miracles and argued for a separation of religion from ethics on the grounds that right conduct is more critical than right doctrine.

Locke became the fountainhead of empiricism, with its epistemology of sensationalism, the use of data gathered through the senses. Before empiricism, Christians had looked for a truth that is true because God knows it as true. With empiricism, truth was judged true because observation showed it to be true (phenomenalism). No longer was the focus on trying to discern what the evidence said about a divine truth that was beyond sight. The empiricist uses deduction to seek an explanation for what the senses say is real. The resulting explanation is tested and accepted, rejected, or refined as it is applied to other situations. Truth has not so much been etched on the mind by God to be discovered by reflection, as it is etched on the sense data that is the basis of knowledge.

The father of skepticism

Scottish historian-philosopher David Hume (1711–1776) accepted empiricism but showed its limitations by arguing that sensual data cannot show with certainty that one thing causes another. People can only accept what their own senses tell them. They cannot know whether the sense information accurately shows what really exists. One implication of this reasoning is that the classical arguments for the existence of God do not necessarily demonstrate his existence. "It is not necessary to believe that effects, such as design, prove the existence of God," Hume argued.

Thus Hume became the father of skepticism. Miracles, one-time occurrences, violate the principle of repeatability and observability; one cannot say they actually happened. "It is contrary to experience that a miracle should be true, but not contrary to experience that testimony should be false," he claimed.

Hume's critique of the power of reason caused several of his countrymen to look for another basis on which to establish religion and ethics. Like the rationalists, the Scottish Common Sense Philosophy placed the guide to life within human faculties, rejecting the idea that sin distorts understanding. According to Thomas Reid (1710–1796), Francis Hutcheson (1694–1746), and Dugald Stewart (1753–1828), among others, the revelation of God has been implanted in common instinct. Knowledge is not experience based; rational processes are shaped by an egalitarian moral intuition.

Jean-Jacques Rousseau (1712–1778).

The German enlightenment

The philosophical critiques of the Germans put them at the forefront of change. Gotthold Ephraim Lessing (1729–1781) argued that the past cannot be known as it happened, time effaces memory, and subjectivity blights perception; therefore Christianity cannot be historically validated. History is separated from observable reality by an "ugly ditch," he suggested, that no contemporary can cross. If the historicity of Christianity cannot be proved, then it must be dismissed.

Lessing reduced Christianity to an essence of moral teachings. In *Nathan the Wise* (1779), he finds truth in all religions—not in their conflicting teachings but in a universal set of moral values they promote.

Immanuel Kant (1724–1804) was the single most important watershed figure in philosophy. His insights utterly changed the way in which philosophy looked at the mind. For Kant, truth was a matter of experience, not revelation.

In *What Is the Enlightenment?* (1784), Kant presented the Enlightenment as an emancipation from immaturity. Maturity meant liberation from such external authorities as Bible, priest, or cleric. Hume's critique of rationalism caused Kant to develop "the critical philosophy." He synthesized contemporary philosophical views to argue that truth is available through an instinctive moral sense and the reason necessary to evaluate. Religion is not found through reason, and certainly it is not found through revelation. The best hope is to see it in a universal moral sense that lies within human perception. In his view, Jesus was a moral ideal for an aspiring humanity.

Deism and Unitarianism: Reason Defines Religion

Deism was an isthmus connecting the philosophical continents of theism and atheism. Like its close cousin, unitarianism, it was designed to rescue religion from its out-of-date ideas. If the medieval-revealed God and religion must be rejected, perhaps faith could be salvaged. Perhaps it was possible to reject atheism, ignorant belief in the Bible, and rationalistic reduction of religion to morality.

In the formulations of Herbert of Cherbury (1583–1648), the founding theologian of the movement; Matthew Tindal (1657–1733); and John Toland (1670–1722), Christian faith was reduced to its most fundamental principles: the existence of God, the necessity of worship, the importance of virtue, sin as moral evil, and expectation of reward and punishment after death. The divine Trinity, deity of Christ, divine justice, moral inability, and blood atonement were set aside as ridiculous and unneeded.

Unitarians

The demarcation between deism and unitarianism is blurred. Deists, such as Benjamin Franklin (1706–1790), viewed God as distant from nature and unconcerned about humanity. They believed God operates in the world through the natural law he established. Thus, they consistently rejected biblical miracles. Unitarians

Sir Isaac Newton (1643–1727). English deists used Newton's discoveries to demonstrate the possibility of a "Natural Religion."

embraced almost the same view of transcendent reality, but they continued to believe that God can and does perform miracles and that some works reported in the Bible happened. God was more personal to unitarians. Thomas Jefferson's (1743–1826) scissor editing of the Bible is an example of the unitarian view; he attempted to remove the corruptions that could not be true from the "pure" text.

The Rise of Pietism and Revivalism

Europe

As a movement, pietism emerged in seventeenth-century Germany in reaction to the decline of religious vitality in the churches. Pietists were distressed as a rationalistic impulse sapped the churches; it seemed that living faith had been replaced by dead creed. The cry of the pietists may have been captured in Blaise Pascal's (1623–1662) dictum, "The heart has its reasons of which reason knows nothing" (*Pensées* 1659, no. 423). The quest for a heartfelt religion, as opposed to dry orthodoxy, caused them to emphasize the emotive and moral aspects of the faith (the necessity of conversion, practical preaching, pastoral care, and evangelism).

The father of pietism

Philip Spener (1635–1705), the "father" of the movement and a Lutheran pastor, wrote the manifesto, *Pious Desires* (1675). Renewal of the church would come, he said, only through a greater emphasis on lay participation, the priority of practice over intellect, and preaching that was edifying and inspiring rather than learnedly doctrinal.

The nursery of pietism was the University of Halle during the tenure of August Francke (1663–1727), a friend of Spener. This professor of theology promoted the creation of a "pietist college" for intense spiritual formation. Foreign missions work was vigorously advanced through creation of the Danish-Halle Mission. Francke also established an orphanage. Revivalist tradition and twentieth-century evangelicalism both had roots in European pietism's program and priorities.

The Moravians

Among Francke's students was Nikolaus von Zinzendorf (1700–1760), a wealthy nobleman. He personally gave refuge to a group of persecuted Christians known as the *Unitas Fratrum* or United Brethren. Under his protection, this group of pietists developed as the Moravian Brethren. The pietistic sect passionately promoted Protestant world evangelization, and Moravian missionaries gave their lives in the first church-sponsored foreign missions effort. Their evangelism effort began in the West Indies in the 1730s.

Blaise Pascal (1623–1662).

Philip Spener (1635–1705).

Britain

The rise of the pietist movement as an antidote to religious decline is evident in the work of such preachers as John Wesley (1703–1791) and George Whitefield (1714–1770). Wesley's heart was "strangely warmed" at a May 24, 1738, Moravian meeting on Aldersgate Street in London. Fired by a passion to renew his church and having visited Zinzendorf in Germany, he was encouraged by his friend Whitefield to reach the masses through field or outdoor meetings.

Wesley and Whitefield

As with Whitefield's mass-evangelism approach, Wesley's labors knew few bounds. Beginning in 1738, he traveled thousands of miles each year and preached several times a week. He desired to bring renewal to the Church of England, but his views separated him from Anglican theology and ecclesiology. Consequently, he organized small societies of believers who met weekly to encourage each other and gathered periodically to hear a traveling circuit preacher.

Under Wesley and Whitefield, winds of renewal swept England, Scotland, and Wales. Whitefield and John Wesley finally parted company when Whitefield's Calvinism became incompatible with Wesley's teaching, which rejected predestination and its foundations in human inability, limited atonement, and eternal security. Wesleyan doctrines embraced a more optimistic view of Christian progress, that Christians could grow to become perfect, in a state of "Holy Love."

Of Wesley's importance in the eighteenth century, his biographer W. H. Fitchett wrote, "He was carried to his grave by six poor men, leaving behind him nothing

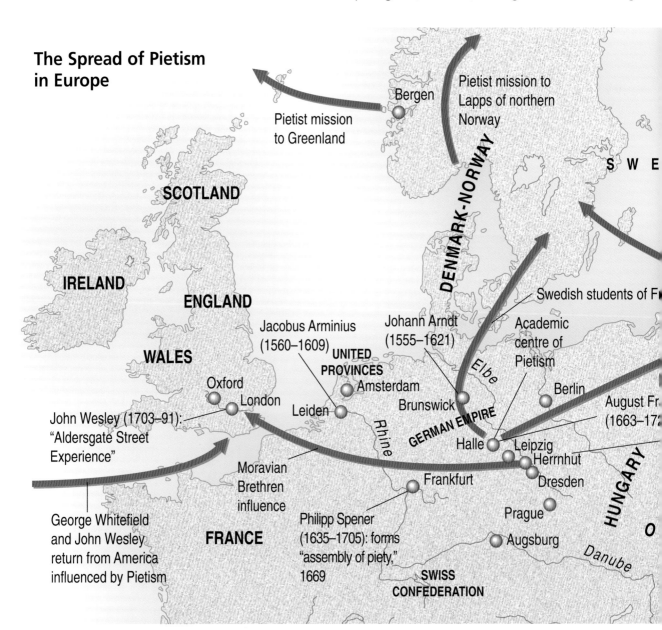

The Spread of Pietism in Europe

Pietist mission to Greenland

Pietist mission to Lapps of northern Norway

Bergen

DENMARK-NORWAY

SWE

SCOTLAND

IRELAND

ENGLAND

WALES

Swedish students of F

Academic centre of Pietism

Johann Arndt (1555–1621)

Jacobus Arminius (1560–1609)

UNITED PROVINCES

Amsterdam

Berlin

August Fr (1663–17:

Oxford
London

Leiden

Brunswick

Elbe

GERMAN EMPIRE

Rhine

Halle

Leipzig

Herrnhut

HUNGARY

John Wesley (1703–91): "Aldersgate Street Experience"

Moravian Brethren influence

Frankfurt

Dresden

Prague

George Whitefield and John Wesley return from America influenced by Pietism

FRANCE

Philipp Spener (1635–1705): forms "assembly of piety," 1669

Augsburg

SWISS CONFEDERATION

Danube

O

John Wesley's birthplace, Epworth, England.

but a good library of books, a well-worn clergyman's gown, a much-abused reputation, and the Methodist Church" (*Wesley and His Century* 1908). After his death in 1791, the British societies formed the English Methodist Episcopal Church in 1795. Wesleyans in the infant United States had originally organized in 1784 to avoid further association with the Church of England. Though John Wesley was a pioneer itinerant, revivalist, and church planter, his brother, Charles (1707–1788) set the movement singing. He, along with Isaac Watts (1674–1748), are the fathers of English hymnody. It has been said that more people were drawn to Methodism by Charles's poetry than by John's preaching.

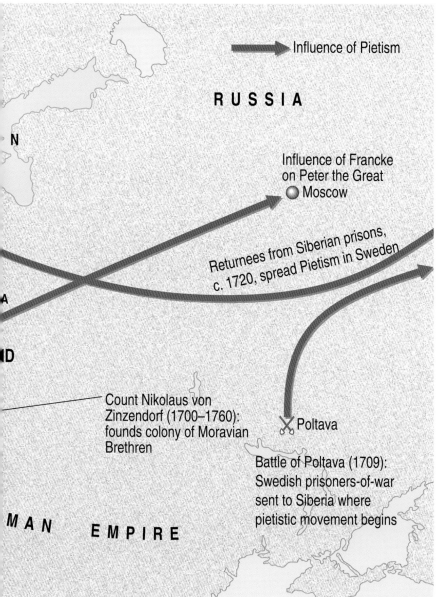

Influence of Pietism

RUSSIA

N

Influence of Francke on Peter the Great
Moscow

Returnees from Siberian prisons, c. 1720, spread Pietism in Sweden

A

D

Count Nikolaus von Zinzendorf (1700–1760): founds colony of Moravian Brethren

Poltava

Battle of Poltava (1709): Swedish prisoners-of-war sent to Siberia where pietistic movement begins

MAN EMPIRE

John Wesley (1703–1791).

British North America

Pietistic renewal was a transatlantic phenomenon. Its strength in the North American colonies dominated by the English demonstrates the interconnection among England's religious community. The awakening began in the 1720s with Theodore Frelinghausen (1691–1747) in the Dutch Reformed community of northern New Jersey. It spread to the Presbyterians, particularly through the innovative Log College pastoral education program developed near Philadelphia by William Tennent (1673–1746) and his son Gilbert (1703–1764). The Log College developed into the College of New Jersey (now Princeton University).

The First Great Awakening

The first home-grown theologian of North America, Jonathan Edwards (1703–1758), was the focal point of religious renewal that engulfed parts of New England in the mid-1730s. The First Great Awakening was in full swing by the early 1740s, partly through the efforts of Edwards but also because of an extensive preaching tour through the colonies by Whitefield. Edwards described the significant ingathering of souls into his own Northampton, Massachusetts, church in *Faithful Narrative of Surprising Conversions* (1737). His numerous writings and sermons went on to define and defend the awakening.

Jonathan Edwards

When he was dismissed as pastor of his church in 1750, Edwards became a missionary among the Native Americans at Stockbridge, Massachusetts. His less strenuous ministry at Stockbridge allowed him to write, defending Christianity against the destructive influence of the Enlightenment. He composed *The Great Doctrine of Original Sin Defended* (1758), *The Freedom of the Will* (1754), and the "Two Treatises": *True Virtue* and *End for Which God Created the World* (1765). He accepted a position as president of the College of New Jersey in 1758 but died of a smallpox vaccination after assuming his duties.

The theology of Edwards indelibly marked the North American church. Edwards's defense of revival was an impetus in the Second Great Awakening in the early nineteenth century. His promotion of Native American evangelism and publication of missionary David Brainerd's diary in 1749 is credited with helping to inspire the explosive outreach of the nineteenth-century world missions movement.

Jonathan Edwards (1703–1758).

George Whitefield (1714–1770).

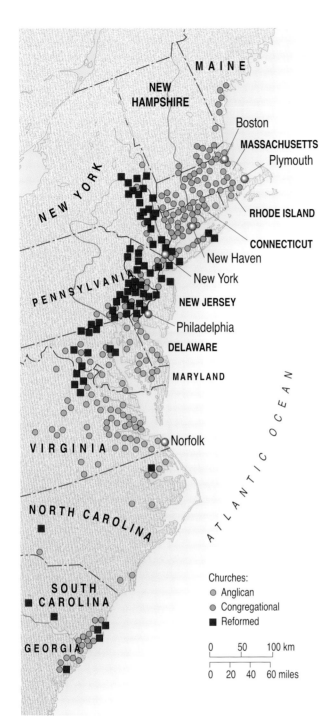

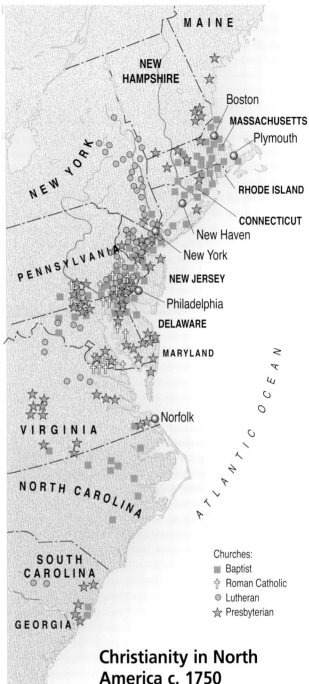

Churches:
- Anglican
- Congregational
- Reformed

0   50   100 km

0   20   40   60 miles

Churches:
- Baptist
- ✝ Roman Catholic
- Lutheran
- ☆ Presbyterian

Christianity in North America c. 1750

Religious enthusiasm

Edwards defended the credibility and validity of movements of awakening from those who would abuse revivals and those who condemned awakenings because of abuses. James Davenport (1716–1757) was a radical enthusiast whose excesses became notorious, but even Whitefield made mistakes that fueled the charge that awakenings were merely the result of uncontrolled emotion.

Critics among the Boston elite churchmen, led by Charles Chauncy (1705–1787), condemned the disorder and intellectual superficiality of awakenings. Against both sides, Edwards developed a groundbreaking theology of the inner direction of the Holy Spirit. In *Religious Affections* (1746), his most important work on the subject, Edwards argued that true religion is neither emotional heat without light nor intellectual light without heat. True works of the Spirit comprise both knowledge and emotion, causing esteem for God. Works of God are essentially known by the resulting true affections of the heart, focused on God and the good of others.

The Rise of European Liberalism and Materialism

Model of a Wesleyan circuit rider.

The southern colonies

In the southern American colonies, Presbyterian revivalists such as Samuel Davies (1723–1761) had significant success in northern Virginia. Anglican Devereux Jarrett (1733–1801) was an enthusiastic awakening preacher in Virginia around the time of the Revolution. He worked closely with Wesley's circuit-rider preachers until Wesleyans cut ties with the Episcopal Church in 1784. Significant Baptist beginnings can be attributed to Shubal Stearns (1706–1771) in North Carolina. Many Separate Baptists, formerly Congregationalists, came out of New England Congregationalism and migrated into the Carolinas.

Some have argued that the Awakening was the first intercolony event, which in some sense prepared the colonists to stand together politically. Whether this is valid, the eighteenth-century revivals had far reaching effect. Conversions appear to have been numerous, and a missionary impulse was directed toward Native Americans and slaves. Several colleges also emerged, including Princeton, Dartmouth (Moor's Indian Charity School), and the University of Pennsylvania (the College of Philadelphia).

The Enlightenment launched a devastating assault on revelation-based medieval conceptions of faith. Europeans gradually reoriented themselves from historic Christian sources of authority to the guidance of autonomous reason. Authority came from within, and faith was directed toward technological progress that promised to bring heaven to earth. Deists and unitarians, following Joseph Priestly's *History of the Corruptions of Christianity* (1782) adopted the belief that God's truth could be found in the Scriptures, but they did not identify the Bible as the Word of God. Lessing anonymously published the *Fragments* of H. S. Reimarus (1694–1768), who accused the writers of Scripture of fraud; he denied the possibility of miracles in the sense recorded in Scripture. Reimarus inaugurated a hitherto unacceptable approach to the Bible.

The insights of Kant into the way knowledge is perceived produced an epistemological devastation. Objectivity was obliterated by the insight that all truth is subjective. Truth is personal and moral. If Kantian theories of truth are valid, Christianity is in crisis, at least as historically envisioned, because Christianity is based on the presupposition of a divine revelation.

The "father" of liberalism

One possible response to this crisis in religion was that of Friedrich Schleiermacher (1768–1834), the "father" of liberal Christianity. Though often interpreted as destructive of Christian faith, he sought to formulate a defense that assumed error in traditional orthodoxy as well as in the theology of the rationalists.

From the perspective of a century later, Barth said that Schleiermacher did not found a school of thought but an era. It was not so much that his religious views were embraced, but his method of approaching assertions of Christianity was appropriated. His twist on Kant was that historical facts are not the basis of religion; religion is the subjective impression that faith-based ideas make upon the conscience. So it matters not whether the historical claims of Christianity are true.

Seeking impregnable ground on which to stand in defense of Christianity, Schleiermacher argued that the essence of religion is an intuitive feeling for God; it is found neither in revelation nor reason. Revelation is a finding of God within the psychological self; it is perception of an eternal reality on which he can lean in dependence. Jesus demonstrates this sense of dependence. His divinity as Christ is actually a heightened perception of his dependence on God. In that sense, the "divine" Christ is a guide to personal self-discovery through religion.

While he made Christianity unfalsifiable if attacked by the rationalist, Schleiermacher disfigured the faith and launched the totally subjective theological quest for the "real" Jesus, as opposed to the one we meet in the Bible. Barth's criticism of this approach is valid. Instead of saving the ship Christianity from its critics, he lost it with all hands aboard.

Theological liberalism

The importance of Georg Hegel (1770–1831) in the development of theological liberalism is monumental. As Hume doubted the classic rational arguments for divine revelation, this Berlin professor demonstrated that history is not static or constant. Historical consciousness is a progressive, evolving experience. An impersonal force in the universe, the Geist, is pushing the human race forward to perfection. Hegel's epistemological bent was to reject anything old and embrace the novel. What was new, after all, was the next step of progress to maturity.

This notion of history allowed the denial of historic doctrines of the faith as simply the "not yet" in a march to perfection. The past as a mere stage of progress became an interpretative tool of vast importance for scholars in many disciplines. Old Testament scholarship soon accepted a progressive development theory choosing among variations of Julius Wellhausen's (1844–1918) JEPD approach. Wellhausen argued for a late development of the Torah by multiple authors representing differing schools of development designated J, E, P, and D: Jahwist; Elohist; Priest; and Deuteronomist.

The Jesus "myth"

David Strauss (1808–1874) shocked Christian thought with the publication of *The Life of Jesus* (1835–1836). Strauss argued that the New Testament tells the myth of a supernatural god-man, created by inspired but deluded men long after the real Jesus lived. Ferdinand Baur (1792–1860) and the theology faculty of the University of Tübingen in Germany explained modern Christianity as the result of a dialectic between the Jewish Christianity of Peter and the Gentile Christianity of Paul. To find real Christianity, one must go beyond the New Testament to the more authoritative second- and third-century sources.

"God is what I eat"

In light of subsequent developments, the work of Ludwig Feuerbach (1804–1872) was particularly impressive. His thought was a precursor to the ideas of Marx and Nietzsche, as well as Sigmund Freud (1856–1939), Martin Heidegger (1889–1976), and Jean-Paul Sartre (1905–1980). Feuerbach argued that religion is a mental creation, even an illness. Whatever God might be, he exists at our behest. Theology is anthropology; it is the human being seeking self-knowledge.

The dictum of Feuerbach, "God is what I eat," became the root of Marx's declaration in *Critique of Hegel's Philosophy of Right* that "Religion is the sigh of the oppressed creature, the heart of a heartless world, just as it is the spirit of a spiritless situation. It is the opium of the people" (1843). To Feuerbach, religion was a human creation; to Marx it was a destructive, debilitating weight that crushed the weak and fearful. Marx saw the human dilemma as rooted in class struggle and the hoarding of wealth by the minority in the capitalistic system. In the hands of Vladimir Lenin (1870–1924) and Leon Trotsky (1879–1940), Marxism became the philosophical basis of the October Revolution in Russia in 1917 and Soviet-style communism as it ruled from 1919

Karl Marx (1818–1883).

Bolsheviks in Moscow, Russia, during the October Revolution of 1917.

to 1989. The quest to create the ideal society through egalitarian economics led to oppression under state-imposed atheism.

Christianity as moral influence

Some churchmen feared that a Christianity based on subjective feelings of need for an unknowable God, and without a foundation in history, could not stand up to the Marxist critique. They sought a more factual basis for faith. Two strategies developed, the moral influence concept pioneered by Albrecht Ritschl (1822–1889) and the comparative religions approach.

Ritschl rejected Hegel's idealism and Schleiermacher's subjectivism. There is a real kingdom of God, he said, though it is unknowably transcendent. The individual reaches for salvation in that reality. Christ connects the individual to the transcendent kingdom. In practical terms, the historic Jesus isn't important, but the moral teachings ascribed to Jesus and the church are vital to bring permanence to the transient human condition. In separating the permanent from the transient, Ritschl reduced the essence of revelation to its moral content. He disregarded the historic, orthodox content.

In Ritschl can be found the fundamental fault line that would crack open Christian faith: the concept that morality is the point of religion. It is assumed that morals can be sustained without an anchor other than a set of approved cultural values.

The most articulate adherent of Ritschlian views was the historian Adolph von Harnack (1851–1930). In *What Is Christianity?* (1900–1901), he argued that the irreducible core of Christian teaching was threefold: (1) the presence of the kingdom of God on earth, (2) the universal fatherhood of God, and (3) the essence of religion in brotherly love. He substituted moral ethic for historic creed.

Christianity—a world religion

The comparative religions approach is called the History of Religions School. Advocates of this approach, such as Wilhelm Bousset (1865–1920), Hermann Gunkel (1862–1932), and Ernst Troeltsch (1865–1923), criticized the Ritschlians for making an arbitrary choice of priorities between moral and doctrinal content in the Bible. The key for comparative religions was the presupposition that all religions share some themes. These commonalities, they reasoned, must be the essence of revelation. Christianity was assumed to be simply one of the world religions and Jesus simply one of the figures who founded a religion. The quest for the true Jesus was to be found in archaeology, not the unreliable texts of Scripture.

The European Reaction to Liberalism

Søren Kierkegaard

Church reaction to these efforts to restructure faith included some insightful thinking but also some serious concessions. Overlooked by contemporaries but important many years later, the Danish recluse Søren Kierkegaard (1813–1855) employed Hegel's method to develop a philosophical ancestor to twentieth-century existentialism. For this reason, he has been scorned by some and given heroic stature by others.

Kierkegaard made a qualitative distinction between God and the finite material universe. Truth cannot be contemplated with rational detachment; it must be embraced subjectively to be true. Though his method was tainted by existentialism, Kierkegaard's valuable point was that truth had to be embraced in the heart. His "leap" for something worth dying for was to the Christ of the Bible.

Objections to higher criticism

Scholars emerged to defend the faith against devastating assaults on Scripture in the social-cultural revolution. German higher criticism had worthy German critics in Johann Neander (1789–1850), Ernst Hengstenberg (1802–1869), and Frederick Tholuck (1799–1877), among others. In England, a pastoral and socially conscious orthodoxy was championed by Brooke Westcott (1825–1901), Fenton J. A. Hort (1828–1892), and Joseph Lightfoot (1828–1889).

In 1880, politician-theologian Abraham Kuyper (1837–1920) and other Dutch Calvinists founded the Free University of Amsterdam, which became the center for a massive conservative revolt from the national Reformed Church. Kuyper became prime minister in 1901 through electoral victories of the Christian Historical Party he had founded. He and Herman Bavinck (1854–1921) left a legacy of voluminous writings that profoundly influenced the evangelical movement.

Austin Henry Layard directs excavations at Nineveh. The nineteenth century saw the beginnings of modern archaeology.

Christianity in Nineteenth-Century England

John Newton (1725–1807), the former slave trader who wrote the hymn text "Amazing Grace."

The fortunes of the Church of England were a portent of the course of religious faith in subsequent centuries. The Roman church in England became the Protestant Church of England in the 1530s under Henry VIII (1491–1547). Elizabeth I (1533–1603), in a reign stretching from 1558 to 1603, institutionalized the national church in what would be its permanent ecclesiastical form. Theoretically the Elizabethan church allowed for considerable diversity of Protestant outlook. In reality, the church was highly polarized and its veneer of unity crumbled into civil war in the 1640s.

High, low, and broad church

The monarchy was restored in 1660, but the Church of England remained too diverse to provide strong spiritual direction. In the nineteenth century, the church was broadly segmented between high church and low church segments. The terms *high* and *low* generally refer to liturgical style and conformist versus nonconformist ways of thinking about church. High church Anglicans also could be divided. The "broad church" group was not a cohesive movement, since it included people who tended to prefer high church liturgy but seldom agreed with one another about theology. Their shared aim was that the church should adapt to theological innovation and reject formal traditions. The broad church group tended toward theology of a Schleiermacher or Ritschl variety.

A London slum in the mid-nineteenth century. Reformers such as Lord Shaftesbury attempted to alleviate poor working conditions.

The Oxford movement

Also part of the high church movement was the Oxford or tractarian movement. Tractarians feared dissolution of authority in a time of rapid change and looked to the church of the patristic and medieval periods for inspiration. To those in the Oxford movement, the ideal church was strong, united, and had Roman Catholic tendencies. John Keble (1792–1866), John Henry Newman (1801–1890), Edward Pusey (1800–1882), and other Anglican clergy became Roman Catholics. Newman became a cardinal.

John Newton

Low church Anglicans were theological conservatives who stressed simplicity and purity. A minority within the Church of England, their faith stressed word and deed, with an overt social consciousness. Among prominent early pastors was John Newton (1725–1807), the former slave trader who wrote the hymn text "Amazing Grace" (1779). Without formal training, Newton was ordained in 1764 and pastored in Olney near London. Newton and his wife opened their home to William Cowper (1731–1800), who suffered from a severe depressive disorder but gave the church some of its great hymns, including "There Is a Fountain Filled with Blood" (1772).

Evangelical Anglicans

Few defenders of traditional theology have exceeded the depth and timeless relevance of John Charles Ryle (1816–1900), an Anglican bishop. Thomas Scott (1747–1821), a biblical commentator, was widely read. Charles Simeon (1759–1836) distinguished himself by developing modern views of small group pastoral care and individual discipleship. Simeon also was a strong promoter of world missions. He had a deep influence on Henry Martyn (1781–1812), whose missionary labors in Persia inspired the church.

The Clapham Sect

The wide-ranging ministries of low churchmen successfully welded social consciousness and conservative theology. A group of influential laymen of the wealthy Clapham district of London formed the Clapham Sect, a benevolent association that funded missions and relief for the poor. A similar group, the Exeter Sect, used political influence to extend missions through the British Empire. William Wilberforce (1759–1833), an aristocratic parliamentarian, labored to end slavery in England and wrote a much-used devotional guide, *Real Christianity* (the condensed name for a much longer title, 1797). Anthony Ashley Cooper, Earl of Shaftesbury (1801–1885), was a tireless advocate for the working poor and helped end child labor abuses. John Howard (1726–1790) spoke

Charles Haddon Spurgeon (1834–1892).

William Booth (1829–1912).

against conditions in England's prisons. Robert Raikes (1735–1811) founded the Sunday school to teach impoverished children to read.

Nonconformists
After the Enlightenment ended Europe's wars of religion, expressions of religion outside the pale of the established Church of England were tolerated without official status. These *nonconformists* included Baptists, Congregationalists, Methodists, Presbyterians, and Roman Catholics.

Plymouth Brethren
There were other churches or parachurch-type missions groups. One of the more successful, the Brethren or Plymouth Brethren,

rejected denominations, the state-church, and an ordained ministry. They gathered in small assemblies or chapels to "break bread" and hear lay elder teachers "break the word." The Brethren sought to practice a pure first-century form of Christianity. A strongly dispensational approach to understanding the Bible developed under the group's nineteenth-century theologians, John Nelson Darby (1800–1882), William Kelley (1821–1906), C. H. Macintosh (1820–1896), and Benjamin Newton (1807–1899).

Two nondenominational organizations emerged to become models for later paraecclesiastical ministries. In 1846, George Williams (1821–1905) founded what became the Young Men's Christian Association (YMCA)

in London. In 1878, former Methodist missionary William Booth (1829–1912) established the Salvation Army. Both agencies excelled in bringing the gospel to the poor and displaced.

Charles Haddon Spurgeon
The most outstanding English preacher of the century was the Baptist Charles Haddon Spurgeon (1834–1892). Thousands attended his services each week at the Metropolitan Tabernacle in Southwark, London. His ministry spawned a college to train pastors, an orphanage, a journal for Christians, and wide literature distribution.

Spurgeon was the most celebrated churchman of his time in England and North America, but his life was troubled by bouts of depression. From 1887 through his death, Spurgeon defended biblical Christianity in a war of words he called the Down Grade Controversy. Spurgeon said liberals had put the gospel on the "down grade." Attempts to redefine the atonement in line with higher criticism of Scripture was at the center of this contentious battle.

Christianity in the New American Nation

The Birth of a Nation

British colonialism ended in the area of North America south of Canada in the Treaty of Paris (1783). Some historians have developed the theory that American colonists sought independence because they accepted an Enlightenment aversion to imposed authority, that the notion of individual rights was applied to the structure of government. Others suggest that incompatible religious visions with the mother country played a significant role. One goal of the Puritan migration across the Atlantic was to establish a divine "city on a hill," a Christian witness before the world. The "evil" state-sponsored church of the motherland threatened the independent religious environment this spirit nurtured.

The United States Constitution

The religious background of the Declaration of Independence and United States Constitution was complex. Founders of the new nation looked to Christianity as moral glue to unite a nation that no longer rallied around a monarchy. The new country would be an association of individual state governments. As originally conceived, states were free to plot their own courses and construct their own rules. Even after the Articles of Confederation (1777; ratified in 1781) were replaced by a strengthened national constitution (1789), minimal authority was vested in the national government. Mainly it would act in the common interests of the diverse state and local governments.

Except for the visionary Alexander Hamilton (1755 or 1757–1804), the first secretary of the treasury, those who designed the government never envisioned that the central government would take priority. With its government by elected state representatives, the nation was to reflect the consensus, while states would cater more narrowly to the will of the people.

Vague about religion

Therefore the Articles of Confederation and the final United States Constitution were intentionally vague about religion. National documents make no reference to Jesus Christ, although he is mentioned profusely in some state documents. In national documents, there is reference to "nature's God," the "Supreme

Signing the U.S. Declaration of Independence, 1776.

21

Judge," and the "Creator." Such conceptions could find assent by a unitarian Thomas Jefferson, a deist Benjamin Franklin, or a trinitarian Roger Sherman (1721–1793). The documents were Christian in orientation to the extent that they confessed God's existence and grounded rights in his sovereignty. However, they went only so far as could be considered a general consensus in that day.

The Implications of the First Amendment

The states-rights orientation of the Articles of Confederation demonstrated that it is easier to foment political dissent than to carry that negative agenda into a functioning government. Painful failures led to creation of a stronger Constitution under James Madison (1751–1836), John Jay (1745–1829), and Hamilton.

To satisfy state concerns, ten amendments were appended to the 1789 constitution. The first guaranteed that equal and unprejudiced treatment would be given to all religious sects, meaning at that time deists, unitarians, Protestants, Roman Catholics, and Jews. The nation was unmistakably Christian in values but only generally God-affirming in governance.

The impact on religion was monumental: Religion was put into a free market economy where the majority rule and individual consent determined its nature. The secular state emerged, embracing no institutional religion and largely rejecting metaphysics, theology, and the possibility of revelation. Egalitarian moral principles of Scottish Common Sense philosophy provided the governing light.

The Second Great Awakening

If the birth of the United States was a radically Enlightenment-oriented political and religious event, how does one account for Protestant hegemony in the subsequent century?

The answer is that conservative Protestants established a majority consensus, a power bloc that captured the public mind. A central reason this consensus became dominant is the Second Great Awakening, which created a Protestant empire. Awakenings stretch through the period before the American Civil War or War Between the States. Unitarianism and deism, so popular in the Revolutionary era, were marginalized in this triumph.

Beginnings

Awakening began in the fears of Protestants, who saw their new country turning to irreligious materialism and expressing considerable approval for the antireligion of the French Revolution. Turning from political dreams of a Christian nation to more transcendent themes, clerics called for concerted prayer and evangelism. Awakening began in the colleges as early as 1789. Yale, Princeton, Hampton-Sidney and other colleges sent awakened graduates back to their churches, and the work spread along the eastern seaboard.

Camp meetings

On the frontier, the locus of revival was in the camp meeting, a gathering of people who came great distances to hear days filled with outdoor preaching. Among those who developed this early mass-evangelism approach was Kentucky Presbyterian evangelist James McGready (1758–1817).

The Second Great Awakening was linked with camp meetings.

The idea was extended to upper New York and into the South. Some meetings were so large and enthusiastic that they frightened those who had started them. One of the most outrageous in conduct was in 1801 at Cane Ridge, Kentucky, under Barton W. Stone (1772–1844). This event was characterized by emotional excess. Awakening-nurtured Protestantism became so strong that religion and national goals became identical throughout the rural areas, which were most of the country.

The impact of this unique approach to religion in a democratic society was not altogether positive. Preaching was reshaped by the need to get people to embrace the faith. As the revival period advanced and became more professionalized, psychological persuasion became important to increasing audience response. Techniques developed that were calculated to trigger inner emotions more than personal confession in the lordship of Christ. Christianity triumphed, but along the way it was culturally compromised.

Charles Grandison Finney

The waves of religious enthusiasm reached a dynamic height in Charles Grandison Finney (1792–1875). His stirring ministry roused the passions, and he directed much of that passion toward social action. As much as anyone, Finney helped build interest in moral reform and missions societies that exploded into existence in the late 1820s. This "Benevolence Empire" prior to the war between northern and southern states (1861–1865) shaped the tradition that characterizes the nondenominational character of modern North American evangelicalism.

Finney was the religious counterpart to his populist contemporary, Andrew Jackson (1767–1845). Both were self-made icons expressing the hopes of the

Charles Grandison Finney (1792–1875).

common man. Finney was the first nationally renowned professional evangelist. He and his followers trooped about the country stirring a nonspecific theology, loose ecclesiastical affiliations, and controversy. They generated heat regarding their methods, theology, and moral platform stressing the end of slavery.

A new theology

Finney was technically an ordained Presbyterian preacher, but he rejected central teachings of Calvinism. He regarded the precise focus on confession and Scripture to be hopelessly antiquated in the new democratic social setting. He wanted more strategic weapons with which to defend the faith against the unitarians, some of whom were dynamic preachers. He carved out a new theology and practices designed as means to conversion.

Foundational to Finney's theology was the belief that sin was a voluntary unwillingness to do what is right. It is basically selfishness and could be remedied by moral resolve, an "I am sorry and promise to do better for God and myself." He denied the fundamental Christian doctrine of absolute inability, subordinated grace to moral resolve, and rejected the substitutionary death of Jesus Christ.

This shifted the emphasis in evangelism from proclamation of God to persuasion of people. He wrote, "The great difficulty is to persuade sinners to choose right. God is ready to forgive them if they will repent; but the great problem is to persuade them to do so." The techniques that became commonplace included protracted meetings, the "anxious bench" to set apart those struggling with their decision, an inquiry room where peer pressure and personal persuasion were used by trained counselors, the public invitation, and organized choirs singing rousing songs. Finney-developed means of

The Chicago evangelist Dwight L. Moody (1837–1899) preaches in London, England.

evangelism are still influential in much of Western Christianity.

Layman's Prayer Revival

A religious wave swept over great segments of the English-speaking world from North America to South Africa in the late 1850s and 1860s. Called the Layman's Prayer Revival of 1858, it began as midday prayer meetings of urban workmen that were usually self-led. It was devoid of the enthusiasm and extremism that characterized much of American religious life. These concerts of prayer began in New York City and spread to other metropolitan areas, and from there into smaller towns. It was largely ended by the coming of civil war in the United States, but already it was spreading from North America to Ireland, Scotland, Wales, and England. From England, it went out to mission stations.

The interdenominational character of this religious movement broke down denominational distinctives. A new configuration of Christian faith was initiated that would finally become the Evangelical Movement.

New Religious Expressions

Creation of a nation emphasizing freedom of conscience placed religion in a new situation. Since all were free to choose the religion they pleased, religionists had to win a following in a free market society. Leaders with charisma attracted adherents; personality had greater trade value than character and cogent teaching. Further, social uncertainties of the new nation led some to seek security in extravagant claims and grand promises.

Utopian communities

Several communal, perfectionistic, utopian communities emerged in this milieu. Foremost among them were the Shakers, followers of the prophet-like Mother Ann Lee (1736–1784). The celibate Shakers gathered into self-supporting communities; practiced various trades, notably furniture making; and anticipated the return of Christ to establish a kingdom on earth.

Another group, the Rappites, were followers of George Rapp (1757–1847). Rapp declared himself "father confessor" and operated his colony with strict regulations. John Humphrey Noyes (1811–1886) established the Oneida Colony in New York. Robert Owen (1771–1858) founded the more secular Harmonites. Most of these social experiments were short-lived.

Four major cults

In addition, the century witnessed the rise of new religion offshoots from Christianity, often referred to as the "four major cults": the Mormons, Seventh-Day Adventists, Jehovah's Witnesses, and Christian Science practitioners. While extremely different from each

Moody's mission partner, the singer Ira D. Sankey (1840–1908).

other, all four were rooted in the democratic soil of tolerance, all centered on a strong figure who demanded strict obedience, and all rejected central Christian teachings.

Commonly, the groups have remained separate from the Christian community by denial of the deity of Christ, redemption through grace as opposed to legal conformity, and blood atonement in Christ. Disciples of these groups believe that they alone are true "saints," with all others outside the fold. They possess their own sacred writings or use Bible-interpretation tools that help disciples reach the correct conclusions.

The Mormons

The Church of Jesus Christ of Latter-day Saints (Mormon) was established on the visions of Joseph Smith Jr. (1805–1844). After the prophet was murdered by a mob, Brigham Young (1801–1877) took the group to the Utah Territory. Mormons believe that Jesus was divine in the same sense in which all people can become God and that God was once a man. Salvation is by law keeping, including the necessity of baptism.

Seventh-Day Adventists

Adventists or Seventh-Day Adventists arose out of the apocalyptic fervor created by William Miller's (1782–1849) penchant for setting calendar dates for the Lord's return to earth. When a second such deadline passed in 1844, he apologized for the trouble he had caused. However, a series of visions, principally reported by Ellen White (1827–1915), soon came along to explain the "Great Disappointment."

Adventists have split into various groups, some orthodox but retaining a Saturday Sabbath. Others followed White, Hiram Edson (1806–1882), or Joseph Bates (1792–1872) into a variety of teachings. White denied Christ's finished work of grace in his death. She embraced the necessity of law keeping, including worship on Saturday, and advocated "soul sleep" between death and the final judgment, and ultimately annihilation of the unbeliever's soul.

Jehovah's Witnesses

Charles Russell (1852–1916) founded the Jehovah's Witness or Zion's Watch Tower Tract Society in 1881. Among its teachings are a denial of the Trinity of God and the deity of Christ. Salvation is through moral rectitude and is reserved for a relative few. The dead go into a state of soul sleep to await judgment, and most of the dead are annihilated or taken out of existence. There is no hell.

Christian Science

Mary Baker Eddy (1821–1910), who had profound health needs herself, taught that pain and death are illusions. She wrote *Science and Health with Key to the Scriptures* in 1875 and formally established the Church of Christ, Scientist in 1879. Her teachings include a belief that humankind is coeternal with God, matter does not exist, Christ is not God, and sin is imaginary. Salvation is the realization that sin does not exist.

A Nation Divided

The War Between the States was a defining point in United States history. The North-South division that led to war was far more complex than the single issue of slavery but slavery was more tangible and emotional than states' rights and economics. Further, the demand for manumission of the slave frequently did not mean that all individuals were viewed as fundamentally equal whatever their race. Jefferson owned slaves as a pragmatic matter. Abraham Lincoln was more interested in advancing federal sovereignty and authority, or limiting authority at the state level, than in abolition. Many Northerners wanted to segregate African-Americans to the Caribbean, on a reservation-like preserve in the Louisiana Purchase territory, or establish more Liberia-type colonies in Africa.

Tension over slavery was evident from the nation's birth. Slavery was banned in the Northwest Territory in 1787. Framers of the Constitution debated slavery but ignored it in the end, except in including a portion of the slave population in determining the apportionment of state representation in Congress. The goal in 1789 was to establish consensus.

The Missouri Compromise

The Missouri Compromise of 1820 established a slavery boundary line across the nation. South of that line, slavery was legal; north of that line, states were "free." There was hope that slave and free states could be admitted to the United States in equal number north and south of what was called the Mason-Dixon Line.

In the 1830s, annexation of part of Mexico became a real possibility. The potential for expanding the reach of slavery showed the hopelessness of permanent compromise. The path to civil conflict escalated rapidly with the potential that the Kansas

President Abraham Lincoln (1809–1865).

General "Stonewall" Jackson (1824–1863).

General Robert E. Lee (1807–1870).

Territory would enter the union as a slave state, although it was above the demarcation line.

The Missouri Compromise was repealed in 1854. When the slave Dred Scott (1795–1858) was taken to live with his master in the free state of Illinois, he filed suit on the ground that a slave could not be owned in a free state. In 1857, the U.S. Supreme Court refused to declare Scott free, a decision that infuriated abolitionists and made withdrawal of Southern states from the national union unavoidable.

The Churches and Slavery

Churches struggled with slavery before the nation as a whole. Samuel Hopkins (1721–1803), a New England clergyman, advocated a recolonization of slaves to Africa. The British created Sierra Leone to repatriate former slaves; the Americans, Liberia. The repatriation experiment proved costly in money and lives, and enthusiasm waned.

Charles Hodge (1797–1878) of Princeton Seminary argued that slaves should be educated to assume a productive place in American society and gradually freed. More radical abolitionists, such as Theodore Dwight

Weld (1803–1895) of Oberlin College and William Lloyd Garrison (1805–1879), demanded immediate manumission. In the Emancipation Proclamation (1863), Lincoln declared immediate manumission for slaves who lived in states then in rebellion. He hoped this declaration would incite slave revolts.

The Southern Baptist Convention

Baptists did not have a centralized governing structure, and their agencies were pledged to neutrality. However, the agencies would not allow slave owners to participate, so Baptists in the South withdrew to form their own regional fellowship in 1845, the Southern Baptist Convention. Baptists in the north continued in a less-structured manner until 1908 when the Northern Baptist Convention was formed.

Presbyterians divide

The dominant Presbyterian denomination, the Presbyterian Church in the U.S.A., divided into New School and Old School wings over theological issues related mainly to revivalism and Calvinism. The 1837–1838 schism was not regional, but the conservative Old School strength was in the South. In 1857, the New School Presbyterian Church,

which was heavily abolitionist, divided geographically over the propriety of slaveholding. The Old School divided after the onset of hostilities. During the war, Southern New School and Old School churches merged into the Presbyterian Church in the Confederate States of America (later renamed the Presbyterian Church in the United States). In 1869 the two northern churches merged to become the Presbyterian Church in the United States of America.

Other denominational groups

Methodists encountered sectional disruption in 1844 over a bishop and a preacher who owned slaves. Their dismissal caused division into the Methodist Episcopal Church North and the Methodist Episcopal Church South.

Other denominational groups did not experience disruption. Congregationalists were exclusively in the north. The Episcopal community had political differences but refused to compromise its theology of the oneness of the body of Christ by dividing. Quakers banned slaveholding before the end of the eighteenth century.

The Emergence of the Foreign Missions Movement

The vitality and growth of Roman Catholic missions after the Reformation was an embarrassment to the gospel-minded Protestants. John Calvin (1509–1564) was one of the first reformers to plant the seed of a Protestant foreign missionary endeavor. Geneva Academy taught and sent teachers and preachers to several nations, and Calvin established the first sending society.

Adrian Saravia (1531–1613) of the Dutch Reformed Church and Justinian von Weltz (1621–1668), a German Lutheran, developed the initial strategy for Protestant missions. Von Weltz was martyred after joining an ill-fated endeavor in Surinam, South America.

The earliest activities

In the age of exploration, as nations competed for economic and commercial supremacy, knowledge of lands and people groups expanded rapidly. As colonial empires were started, trading companies sent clergy to minister to the colonials who went to the foreign lands to live and work. This was the earliest form of modern missions. Then missions societies not connected with the trading companies were established to reach foreign nationals. The Walloon Synod of the Dutch Reformed Church (1644), the Church of England's Society for the Propagation of the Gospel in Foreign Parts (1701), and the Scottish Society for Propagating Christian Knowledge (1707) began. The Danish-Halle Mission (1704) created a school specifically to train missionaries, who were sent to India.

The Moravians took on missions as a primary focus. In a prayer meeting in 1732 the Spirit of God seemed to call them specifically to this endeavor. Within a generation they had sent missionaries throughout the world.

The "Birth" of Modern Missions

The mission of William Carey (1761–1834) to Madagascar and India in 1792 established a new era in missions from English-language countries. Carey's work was under the newly created Particular Baptist Society for Propagating the Gospel to the Heathen. Ecclesiastical denominations were inaugurating the great century of Protestant foreign missions. Agencies proliferated, including the London Missionary Society (1795), the Glasgow and Edinburgh Missionary Society (1796), the Church Missionary Society (1799), the Basel Missionary Society (1816), and the Berlin Missionary Society (1824). The nations began to hear.

U.S. missions

Churches in the United States became involved as news of mission successes filtered back. The most celebrated U.S. missions beginning was an impromptu 1806 prayer gathering of some students at Williams College in western Massachusetts as they huddled under a haystack during a rainstorm. Several students at the Haystack Prayer Meeting went on to serve abroad, among them Adoniram Judson (1788–1850). A vigorous promoter of missions was another Haystack Prayer Meeting participant, Samuel J. Mills (1783–1818). These men appealed to Congregationalist leaders and in 1810 formed the

Pioneering missionary William Carey (1761–1834) points out India on a leather wall map.

C. T. Studd (1860–1931), English cricketer and founder of the Heart of Africa Mission, which later became the Worldwide Evangelization Crusade.

David Livingstone (1813–1873), Scottish missionary and explorer.

American Board of Commissioners for Foreign Missions. Judson and Luther Rice (1783–1836) were the first to be sent out; they sought to join Carey's work. Judson went on to do his major work in Burma.

Because Judson and Rice came to Baptist views on baptism, they felt compelled to separate from the American Board. Consequently, Baptists formed the American Baptist Missionary Union (1814) to support them. Presbyterians formed the

The first party of China Inland Mission workers in 1866.

Presbyterian Board in 1837 during the New School–Old School schism. Previously, individual presbyteries had been actively sending out missionaries.

The "Faith Missions Movement"
A new direction of missions endeavor emerged, the nonde-nominational or independent missions board. These were called faith missions because they operated without denominational financial support. Englishman J. Hudson Taylor (1832–1905) founded China Inland Mission in 1865 (now Overseas Missionary Fellowship International). His missionary endeavors became a model for others. H. Grattan Guinness (1835–1910) founded Livingstone Inland Mission (1870; now Africa Inland Mission). Albert Simpson (1843–1919) established the Christian and Missionary Alliance (1886). C. I. Scofield (1843–1921) organized the Central American Mission (1890).

Hundreds of dedicated pioneer missionaries labored to lay a foundation for later harvests. Most worked, and many died, in obscurity. Another great surge in missions would come after World War II.

The U.S. Church Post–Civil War

The Gilded Age

The post-war Gilded Age was an unprecedented period of economic prosperity in the United States. The era began as the continent was spanned by the railroad and closed with emergence of the automobile industry.

This era signaled the new status of the United States as a world power. Thomas Alva Edison (1847–1931) invented the incandescent bulb; William Graham Bell (1847–1922) perfected the telephone. It was the era of the rail and steel, of Jay Gould (1836–1892), Andrew Carnegie (1835–1919), and John D. Rockefeller (1839–1937). Cities mushroomed; the prairie was cultivated as 160-acre tracts of land were allotted free under the Homestead Act of 1862. Conversely, there were two presidential assassinations and economic downturns in the 1870s and 1890s. Violent labor-management clashes shocked the nation in the Great Railroad Strike (1877), Gould Railway and Haymarket strikes (1886), Homestead Steel Mill Strike (1892), and Pullman Railroad Strike (1894). Unions emerged to protect the worker from unscrupulous robber barons.

There were other unsettling trends. Cheap housing created the inner-city slum when immigrants swarmed into cities for available, low-wage work. The immigrants from Europe's southern Roman Catholic countries threatened the Anglo-Saxon Protestant myth of supremacy. America was a nation in the midst of change.

Natural science and religion

The most far-reaching change in American life undoubtedly surrounded the relationship between natural sciences and religion. The Enlightenment had installed a firmly secularized culture. The hold of Second Great Awakening Protestant Christianity, weakened by sectional conflict, was about to fracture and collapse in the United States, even though outward manifestations of religion continued to prosper.

The root of religious change took place between 1880, when the battle became evident, and 1930, when the triumph of Scottish Common Sense and Enlightenment reason over faith in the supernatural seemed complete. Scientific advances and theories promised to explain through natural processes all that had been explained by religion.

Advertisement for Edison-Bell phonograph, 1900.

Wright brothers' plane at Le Mans, France, in 1908.

Charles Darwin (1809–1882).

Sigmund Freud (1856–1939).

Darwinism

Charles Darwin (1809–1882) did not cause this battle, but he contributed to it. The discussion of developmentalism within the species is as old as the Greeks. Comte de Buffon (1707–1788), Jean Lamarck (1744–1829), and Robert Chambers (1802–1871) popularized it once again. Chambers's *Vestiges of Creation* (1844), promoting natural selection as God's method of creation, was discussed in Boston's intellectual circles.

The difficulty, however, was that no natural mechanism seemed to explain mutations that caused momentous changes in species. Darwin came up with a plausible idea that demand for food was greater than the available supply. Many believed that he had removed the last argument for theism. Design did not require a designer. What was needed was vast periods of time and favorable conditions for progressive mutation.

Evolution became the Rosetta Stone that could be applied to advance many emerging disciplines, even outside the hard sciences in fields such as sociology or psychology, from Sigmund Freud to the behaviorist John Broadus Watson (1878–1958). Theistic creation assertions were displaced by naturalistic and environmental explanations to explain anything from the origin of the universe to criminal actions by people.

For Christians, it was a monumental crisis: How could faith be maintained in a scientific age? Theologians began to shift away from the Bible to accommodation. Faith was reframed around assumptions of developmental science and the modern antisupernatural spirit. Tensions increased between those who believed that change was necessary and those who saw the substantive changes being advanced as a betrayal.

The New Theology

One popular approach to preserving Christian faith through change was the New Theology. The endeavor can be criticized for surrendering too much that was essential. The intent, though, was an honest attempt to respond to rationalistic attacks on faith with a rationalistic version of Christianity. What they ended up erecting was a blighted theology that became a truncated perversion of the real thing.

The New Theology that would come to be known as liberal or modernist Christianity followed the lead of German theologians, with the work of Ritschl dominant. They sought to separate truth from error in the Bible, the permanent from the transitory, to restore the "true" Christian message. This truth would be comfortably safe from the attacks of rationalists, materialists, and archaic traditionalists.

The key was Jesus, according to William Newton Clarke (1841–1912), the first in this tradition to publish a systematic theology. Material in the Bible congenial to what was identified as the "spirit of Jesus" was valid. The rest was not. However, Clarke acknowledged Jesus as a Jewish peasant with impeccable morals and amazing insight into human nature. His divinity was no more or less than that of the rest of the human race.

The essence of Christian faith was to follow the moral example of this teacher. In place of Christ's supernatural claims was faith in the progressive perfecting of human nature through education. Evolution was embraced, along with a naive do-good-ism.

On the Brink of Disintegration

All of the factors were in place to make the twentieth century a most interesting series of decades. This period will be covered in a more detailed overview in volume 6 of this series. Ironically, the twentieth century would be one of the most significant eras for the expansion of Christian faith through the world. Western Christianity would play less and less of a role as the philosophical dominance of rationalism became absolute—and then began to disintegrate rapidly.

The twentieth century also witnessed the crumbling of liberal Christianity's ideal of a morally evolving human species. Liberated from medieval authority structures and set on a path of self-discovery, leaders during the early century embraced the notion that human nature could be educated and programmed into civility. The resulting world would be increasingly safe from wars, disease, and want.

An age of horror

Instead, incivility reached previously unimagined levels of cruelty and murderous disregard for life. At the center of each example of horror were elitists who took evolution-based political philosophies to demonic but logical conclusions.

A sampling of these events must include: 1.5 million Armenians, killed by the Ottoman Turks (1915); 7–9 million Ukrainians and millions more elsewhere murdered in Josef Stalin's agrarian reform (1932–33); as many as 600,000 Chinese purposely killed in the Japanese invasion (1937–38); at least 6.5 million Jews and 5 million from other populations destroyed in the Nazi Holocaust (primarily 1938–45); 2 million Cambodians killed by the Khmer Rouge (1975–79); 200,000 murdered in Bosnia-Herzegovina by Serbian nationalist Slobodan Milosevic (1992–95); 800,000 Tutsis dead from Hutus efforts in the Rwandan civil conflict (1994).

The collapse of modernism

World wars and international conflicts brought an end to the facile optimism of Enlightenment rationalism. Modernity collapsed under the weight of critiques by nihilism, existentialism, and finally postmodernism. A materialist "live-now" attitude made entertainment and titillation a preoccupation of the West.

But the twentieth century also was the century of explosive Christian expansion through the Pacific Rim, China, Africa, and South America. Technology contributed wonderful new opportunities for Christianity in the world, from air travel to computer chips and satellite communications. This series will next look closely at this uncertain but dynamic period for faith.

Adolf Hitler (1889–1945).

Japanese Emperor Hirohito in 1942.

Mao Tse Tung (1893–1976).

Index